THE WORLD OF PLANTS

HOW DO ANIMALS HELP PLANTS REPRODUCE?

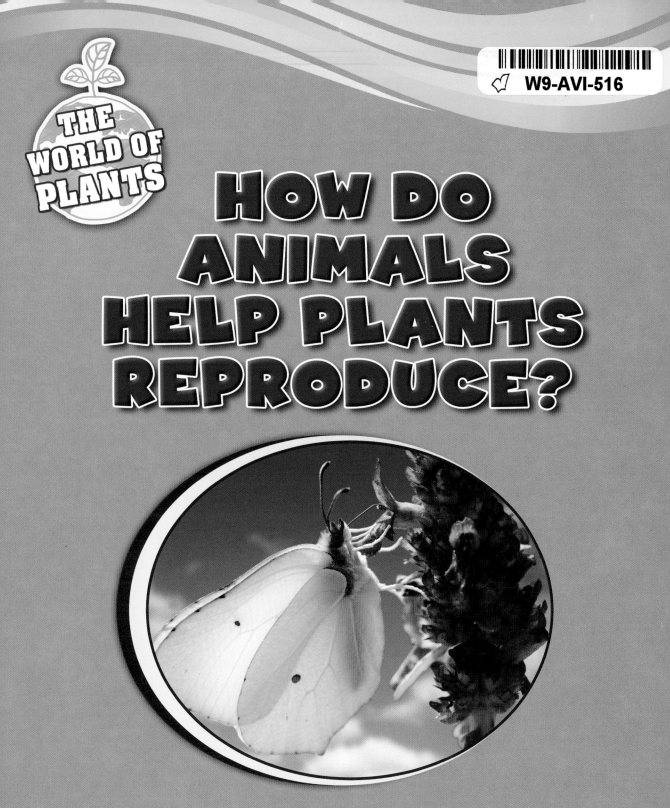

by Ruth Owen

PowerKiDS
press

New York

Published in 2015 by The Rosen Publishing Group, Inc.
29 East 21st Street, New York, NY 10010

First Edition

Produced for Rosen by Ruby Tuesday Books Ltd
Editor for Ruby Tuesday Books Ltd: Mark J. Sachner
US Editor: Joshua Shadowens
Designer: Emma Randall

Photo Credits:
Cover, 1, 4–5, 6–7, 8–9, 10–11, 12–13, 14–15, 16–17, 18–19, 20–21, 22–23, 25 (top), 26–27, 28–29 © Shutterstock; 24, 25 (bottom) © FLPA.

Library of Congress Cataloging-in-Publication Data

Owen, Ruth, 1967–
 How do animals help plants reproduce? / by Ruth Owen. — First edition.
    pages cm. — (The world of plants)
 ISBN 978-1-4777-7141-9 (library binding) — ISBN 978-1-4777-7142-6 (pbk.) —
ISBN 978-1-4777-7143-3 (6-pack)
 1. Pollination—Juvenile literature. 2. Animal-plant relationships—Juvenile literature. I. Title. II. Series: World of plants (New York, N.Y.)
 QK926.O94 2015
 571.8'642—dc23
                            2014009563

Manufactured in the United States of America

CPSIA Compliance Information: Batch #WS14PK8: For Further Information contact Rosen Publishing, New York, New York at 1-800-237-9932

Contents

It's All About Teamwork

If you've ever sat near a colorful flowerbed in a garden or park on a warm summer day, you may have heard a chorus of buzzing noises. The noise is being made by bees.

It's easy to take bees for granted and not even notice them busily diving in and out of flowers. What's going on, however, is a perfect example of natural teamwork.

The bees are hard at work gathering food made by the flowers. As the bees do this, they are making it possible for the plants to **reproduce**.

Bees aren't the only animals that help plants in this way. Insects, birds, bats, and many other animals help plants produce their **seeds**. Once a plant has produced seeds, some animals even act as nature's gardeners by spreading the seeds!

A Flower Up Close

Many **species** of plants reproduce by growing flowers that make seeds.

While flowers come in lots of different shapes and sizes, all flowers have the same parts for reproduction. A flower has petals that may be colorful, scented, or a special shape to attract the animals that will help with reproduction.

A Crocus flower

Stigma

Anther with pollen

Crocuses growing in the woods in spring

Inside a flower are male and female parts. The male parts are called **stamens**. Each stamen is made up of a thin stalk called a filament and an **anther** that produces a dust called **pollen**. The female part of a flower is called the **pistil**. The pistil is made up of an **ovary**, which is deep inside the flower, a stalk called a **style**, and a part called the **stigma**, which is often sticky. Some types of flowers have just one pistil, while others have several pistils.

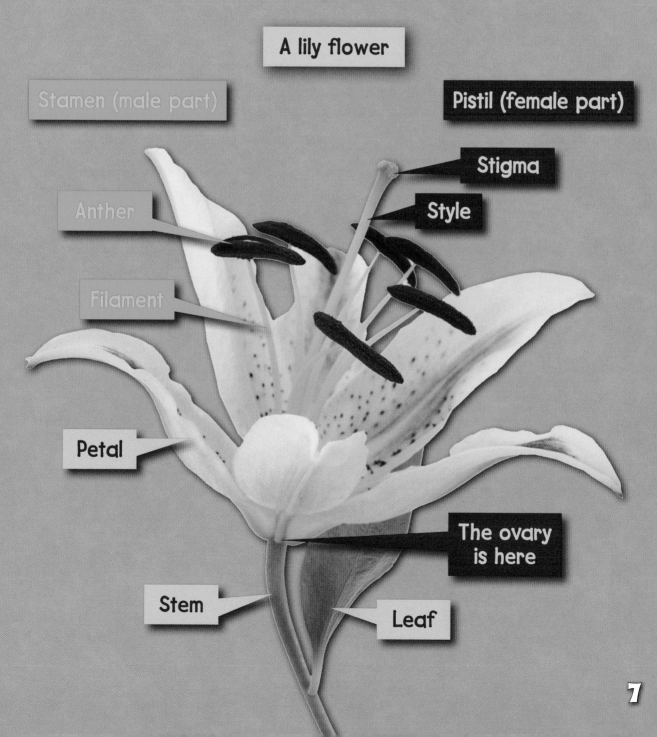

A lily flower

Stamen (male part)

Pistil (female part)

Stigma

Anther

Style

Filament

Petal

The ovary is here

Stem

Leaf

Once a plant's flowers have produced pollen on their anthers, the process of reproducing, or making seeds, can begin.

For most plants, to get this process started, pollen from the anthers of one flower must be carried to the stigma of another flower. This happens with the help of animals such as honeybees.

To attract honeybees and other tiny animal visitors, flowers produce a sweet liquid called **nectar**. Honeybees visit flowers to drink nectar.

Anthers

Honeybee

Pollen

As a honeybee crawls around inside a flower searching for its sweet treat, pollen from the flower's anthers sticks to its fuzzy body.

When it has finished feeding at one flower, the bee flies to a different flower. The pollen that's stuck to the bee goes too!

A Special Delivery

Carrying its load of pollen, a honeybee lands on a different flower.

Once again, the bee crawls around inside the flower searching for nectar to drink. As the bee moves around, pollen from its body brushes off inside the flower.

Pollen

Some of the pollen sticks to the flower's stigma. Now the process of making seeds can begin for the flower. When pollen from one flower's anthers is transferred to the stigma of another flower, it's called **pollination**.

A bee doesn't deliberately **pollinate** flowers. As the bee looks for food, the whole process happens without the insect knowing.

Stigma

Lily

All About Pollination

Flowers can only be pollinated by pollen from a plant of the same species. For example, a lily could never be pollinated by pollen from a daffodil.

Most flowers do need to be cross-pollinated, though. This means they need pollen from their own species, but from a different flower. This is why bees are so helpful. A bee may carry pollen between two flowers that are several feet (m) apart, or even several miles (km) apart. Lilies are a type of plant that must be cross-pollinated.

The parts of a tomato flower

Petal

Anthers

Stigma

Other plants, such as tomato plants, however, are self-pollinators. This means pollination can take place if the flower's own pollen lands on its own stigma. Sometimes this happens inside a tomato flower without help. Usually, though, pollen gets moved around inside the flower on the body of a bee or other insect.

A bee pollinating a tomato flower

Making Seeds

Once a flower has been pollinated, it's time for fertilization to take place.

This begins with the pollen grains that are stuck to the flower's stigma. A pollen grain sends a tiny tube down the flower's style from the stigma into the ovary. Inside the ovary are **ovules**, which are tiny plant parts that can become seeds. The pollen tube pierces an ovule and fertilizes it. Now the ovule can grow into a seed.

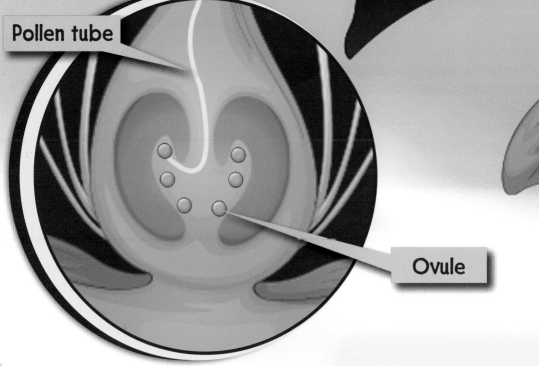

Pollen tube

Ovule

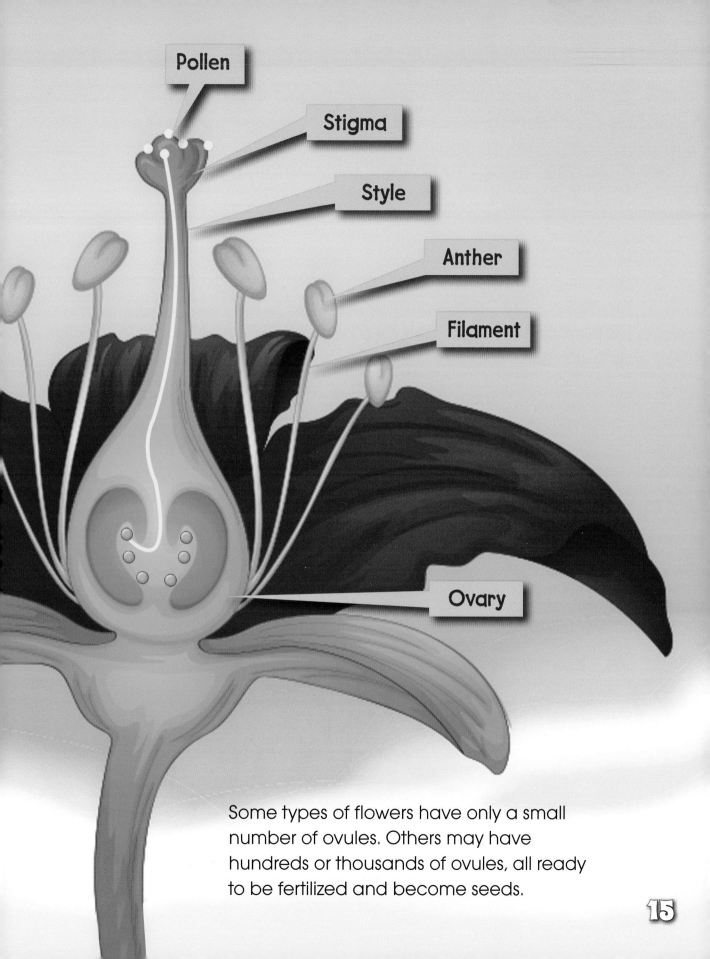

Pollen

Stigma

Style

Anther

Filament

Ovary

Some types of flowers have only a small number of ovules. Others may have hundreds or thousands of ovules, all ready to be fertilized and become seeds.

A Perfect Partnership

As bees pollinate flowers, they obtain nectar and pollen.

Flowers direct bees to their nectar by giving the insects guidelines to follow on their petals. These guidelines are invisible to humans because they only reflect ultraviolet light. Humans cannot see ultraviolet light. Bees see these types of light waves as colors, however.

Honeybees feed on the nectar they find. They also carry it back to their hives where it is made into honey. Bees eat honey and store it as a food source for the winter.

Honeybee

Pollen basket

Some of the pollen that sticks to a bee's body is spread from flower to flower. The rest is collected in body parts called pollen baskets and is carried back to the hive. Here, the pollen is made into food that is fed to bee **larvae** and young bees.

Bees store honey in honeycomb inside a beehive.

Honeycomb

Honeybees

Honey

Bees and Our Food

A honeybee visits up to 5,000 flowers in a single day. Worldwide, bees pollinate billions of plants every year.

It's not only lilies and other pretty garden plants that need bees. Without bees it would be impossible for farmers to grow many food crops.

Trees that produce fruits such as apples, oranges, cherries, and peaches are pollinated by bees. Foods such as tomatoes, zucchini, and beans rely on bee pollination. So do peanuts, almonds, coffee, and herbs. Bees also pollinate crops such as clover and alfalfa that are fed to cattle that supply us with milk and meat.

Almond tree flower

Almonds

It's been estimated that about one-third of the foods we eat come from plants that are pollinated by bees.

A field of alfalfa

It's not only bees that help plants reproduce. Many other species of insects help with this important task, too.

Butterflies, moths, lacewings, beetles, and even wasps all act as pollinators when they visit flowers to drink nectar. A butterfly or moth can drink nectar that other insects cannot reach using its long straw-like tongue, called a proboscis. As the insect gently flutters from flower to flower drinking nectar, it spreads pollen with its body and wings.

Proboscis

A sphinx moth drinking nectar

A lacewing

Not all insects eat nectar. Some species of flies feed and lay their eggs on animal waste or rotting flesh, called carrion. These insects can still help pollinate flowers, though. To attract carrion flies to their petals, some flowers produce scents that smell like rotting meat or dog waste!

This carrion flower produces a smell like rotting meat to attract pollinators.

Bird Pollinators

Many plants rely on birds to pollinate their flowers.

Around the world, about 2,000 different species of birds eat nectar, or visit flowers to hunt insects that feed on nectar. Hummingbirds, honeycreepers, honeyeaters, sunbirds, and parrots all act as pollinators while feeding at flowers.

A hummingbird drinking nectar from a hibiscus flower

Plants that are pollinated by birds don't use scent to attract their pollinators. This is because most birds do not have a strong sense of smell. Bird-pollinated plants often have large, brightly colored, trumpet-like, or funnel-shaped flowers. The large flowers allow birds, such as hummingbirds, to dip their beaks, heads, or sometimes their whole bodies, deep into the flower. When the bird has finished drinking nectar, it flies away from the flower with pollen stuck to its feathers.

A sunbird drinking nectar

It's not just insects and birds that work as pollinators. Some species of lizards carry out this task. Some mammals also transport pollen on their furry bodies.

Many plants are pollinated at night by bats. These flying mammals visit flowers to drink nectar and eat pollen. They also visit flowers to hunt for nectar-feeding insects. About 300 different species of fruit-producing plants depend on bats as pollinators. These include bananas, guavas, and mangoes.

On the island of Madagascar, black-and-white ruffed lemurs pollinate the traveler's palm tree as they feed on its nectar. In Australia, mouse-sized honey possums eat pollen and nectar with their long tongues. These tiny mammals enable many flowering plants to reproduce.

A honey possum

A black-and-white ruffed lemur

A bat drinking nectar

Nature's Gardeners

Once a flower has been pollinated and produces seeds, it sometimes needs help from animals in another way.

Flowers grow their seeds in protective cases, or fruits, such as berries. A bird or other animal may feed on the fruit and swallow the seeds. The seeds then travel through the animal's **digestive system**, often without being harmed. When the animal then goes to the bathroom some time later, the seeds leave its body in its waste. By this time, the animal may be far from the plant that produced the seeds. Without realizing, the animal has helped the plant spread its seeds to new growing places.

A squirrel monkey eating papaya

All around us this amazing example of teamwork is taking place every day. Plants produce food for animals, and in return, animals pollinate the plants and help them spread their seeds.

Cedar waxwings eating berries

Investigating the World of Plants

You will need:

- A notebook and pencil
- A magnifying glass
- A watch (or other device for timing one minute)
- A camera

Go Pollinator Watching

On a warm, dry, spring or summer day, find some flowers and go pollinator watching. The flowers can be wildflowers or weeds, or plants growing in a garden or park. Here are some fun activities to try.

BE CAREUL! When insect watching do not touch the bees or other insects, or put your face close to them. Watch the insects at work without disturbing them. Always go pollinator watching with an adult.

Get Up Close

Hold a magnifying glass close to a flower. Can you identify its anthers and stigma? Can you see the flower's pollen?

A flowerbed in a park

Bee Count

Count the number of bees on each type of plant. Do the bees seem to prefer some colors over others? Do the preferred flowers have a more powerful scent than the other flowers?

Bee Time Trial

Use the second hand on a watch to time a bee for one minute. How many flowers does the insect visit in that time?

Thousands of Bees

Look closely at the bees on the flowers. Do they all look the same? There are about 4,000 different species of bees in North America. You can research the different types of bees that live in your state at the library or online.

Honeybee   Bumblebee   Valley carpenter bee

Butterflies and Other Pollinators

Do you see butterflies or other pollinators on the flowers? How many different insects can you spot? Are the butterflies visiting the same flowers as the bees?

There are more than 700 different species of butterflies in North America. You can take photos of the butterflies you see, then check out what species they are by looking online or using a butterfly guide from the library.

Common North American Butterflies

Great spangled fritillary   Red admiral   Common buckeye   Red-spotted purple

Spicebush swallowtail   Monarch   Eastern tiger swallowtail

Glossary

anther (AN-thur)
The part of a flower that produces pollen.

digestive system
(dy-JES-tiv SIS-tem)
The group of body parts, including the stomach and intestines, that break down food so that a body can use it for fuel.

larvae (LAHR-vee)
The young of many types of insects. A larva hatches from an egg.

nectar (NEK-tur)
A sweet liquid, produced by flowers, that many insects and other animals eat.

ovary (OH-vuh-ree)
The part of a flower where its seeds form.

ovules (AHV-yuhlz)
Tiny parts of a plant that become seeds when fertilized by pollen.

pistil (PIS-tuhl)
The female reproductive part of a flower. The pistil is made up of the ovary, the style, and the stigma.

pollen (PAH-lin)
A colored dust made on the anthers of flowers, which plants need in order to reproduce.

pollinate (PAH-luh-nayt)
To move pollen from the anthers of one flower to the stigma of another.

pollination
(pah-luh-NAY-shun)
When pollen is moved from the anthers of one flower to the stigma of another.

reproduce (ree-pruh-DOOS) To make more of something, such as when plants make seeds that will grow into new plants.

seeds (SEEDZ) Parts of a plant that contain all the material needed to grow a new plant.

species (SPEE-sheez) One type of living thing. The members of a species look alike and can reproduce together.

stamens (STAY-munz) The male parts of a flower. Each stamen is made up of a filament and an anther.

stigma (STIG-muh) The part of a flower where pollen must land in order for pollination to happen so that a flower can begin to make seeds.

style (STYL) Part of a flower's pistil. The style is a stalk that connects the stigma to the ovary.

Websites

Due to the changing nature of Internet links, PowerKids Press has developed an online list of websites related to the subject of this book. This site is updated regularly. Please use this link to access the list:

www.powerkidslinks.com/wop/repro/

Read More

Linde, Barbara M. *The Life Cycle of a Honeybee*. New York: Gareth Stevens, 2011.

Thomson, Ruth. *A Sunflower's Life Cycle*. New York: PowerKids Press, 2010.

Waldron, Melanie. *Flowers*. Mankato, MN: Capstone Press, 2014.

Index